MUSHROOMS FOR DINNER
A German girl survives World War II

Brigitta Day
With an epilogue by her son, Peter

Copyright © Brigitta Day and The Expressive Press, 2020. All rights reserved. No part of this book may be reproduced or transmitted in any form or by any means, whether electronic or mechanical, including photocopying, recording or by any information storage and retrieval system, without the written permission of the author and publisher.

The Expressive Press
www.TheExpressivePress.com

ISBN: 9798669916800

Memory: The power to revive again in our minds those ideas which, after imprinting, have disappeared, or have been, as it were, laid aside, out of sight.

– John Locke, 1689,
English philosopher
whose *Two Treatises of Government*
proposes a more civilized society.

Pictures made in childhood are painted in bright hues.

– Kate Douglas Wiggin, 1886,
an American educator and author of children's stories,
most notably the classic children's novel
Rebecca of Sunnybrook Farm.

Table of Contents

Foreword: A contemporary view from America
Two home fronts, two ways of life............................... 7

Chapter 1: 1938–1943: My first five years in Leipzig
The war turned this thriving cultural center into a wasteland of terror and despair...................................... 9

Chapter 2: Winter 1943– winter 1944: A short stay in friendly Wittichenau
Making a life in cramped conditions............................ 31

Chapter 3: 1944–1964: We escape to Bavaria and start a new life
An oasis of peace amid chaos 45

Chapter 4: I return to Leipzig
After the war ended I found a few new buildings, others in ruins, many bullet holes, and polluted air and water.. 81

Epilogue: A Note from Peter Day...................................... 86

Foreword: A contemporary view from America

Two home fronts, two ways of life

As a young American only five years older than Brigitta Day, my memories of WW II are far different than hers. She lived WW II. I heard about it from the radio reports of such journalists as Ernie Pyle, Edward R. Murrow, and Gabriel Heater. Yes, the reports scared me with their horror that I was forced to visualize. Without question, it was a long way from being there, as Brigitta was.

In her graphic monologue, Brigitta describes life on the home front of Germany during the six years of WW II. It wasn't easy compared to mine.. While she was scavenging for food in the woodlands of Saxony and Bavaria, my family and millions of other Americans were shopping in super markets adequately stocked with the basics of life while complaining quietly about the lack or scarcity of certain items such as sugar and meat. While she was huddling in basements to protect herself and her family from Allied bombs, Americans along the East coast, especially in the New York Metropolitan Area where I lived, were gathered in darkened basements to survive air raids by German bombers that, thankfully, never materialized. While her Father, in his early fifties, was conscripted into the German army and was subsequently killed in battle for a cause that he vehemently opposed, my Father, only a few years younger, was employed as an engineer and living with his family in a quiet suburb.

Brigitta's story amplifies the reasons, the hopes—if any are needed by sane people everywhere—that there will never be another war.

– Pete Geissler,
Brigitta's friend and publisher

Chapter 1: 1938–1943:
My first five years in Leipzig

The war turned this thriving cultural center into a wasteland of terror and despair

New City Hall of Leipzig, built in 1905

I remember Leipzig as a city of beauty some 115 miles southwest of Berlin, an enormous expanse over flat land, with seemingly unending streets and boulevards, streetcars with soft bell sounds connecting it all. The sidewalks were wide and lined with planters. There were green spaces and parks everywhere. More than half a million people lived in well-established neighborhoods. In the center where my grandparents and aunts lived, the railroad station, an impressive structure by size and design, stood in the middle of Augustusplatz which connected the train system to streetcars.

Augustusplatz with Leipzig Opera House, c. 1900

There were many publishing companies as Leipzig was the place where the largest book fair took place yearly. Music played a large role in Leipzig; it was the home of the famous Gewandhaus Orchestra and an opera house.

New Gewandhaus - Concert Hall from 1884-1944

Thomaskirche in the city center had attracted attention since Johann Sebastian Bach spent 40 of his most productive years there as choirmaster, conductor and composer. Felix Mendelson filled the same post about 100 years later and brought renewed attention to Bach's music and his own compositions.

Thomaskirche Church, c. 1885.
Home to the Thomanerchor, this church was partially damaged during Allied bombing raid on Leipzig, later requiring repair.

Leipzig was also the home of the Thomanerchor, a boys' choir that was widely known for singing hymns and religious carols. In those early years, classical music was not on our horizon, but opera and the children's theatre gave me the feeling of living in a dream world. I remember

Leipzig in so many details because these early years were my happy years, full of love and family in beautiful surroundings; I was an adult before I found comfort and happiness again.

First Grandchild for the Bedrich Family. From the left, my Grandmother, Aunt Angela, Grandfather holding me in his arms, Mother and Aunt Magda

I was born on February 19, 1938, as the first grandchild in a large family of one set of grandparents and many aunts. It was the year British Prime Minister Chamberlain met Hitler in Munich and offered peace. Hitler had already annexed an area called Sudetenland, part of Bohemia.

In a Park in Leipzig with my Mother, c. 1938

My father, my mother and I on a family vacation, c. 1938

My brother Wolfgang came along less than two years later, on December 4, 1939, just as World War II started with the invasion of Poland by Hitler. We lived in a part of town outside of the central area, not the finest, Aunt Magda would say.

*Wolfgang, my brother, was born in 1939.
He loved to take rides in the baby carriage in parks.*

My Father had grown up in this neighborhood and had real estate holdings in the area. One of them was his Father's former window factory, a small building on a corner lot. We occupied a large apartment on the fifth floor of a building. It was furnished in old dark wood pieces; my mother only had interest in her family and never attempted to change the décor. A winding staircase lined with stained glass windows connected the floors and there was a wrought iron enclosed elevator but I cannot recall that it ever worked. In the back of the apartment building there was a paved courtyard where children would play and there were also small plots for tenants to grow vegetables and flowers.

Writing my first book in 1940 in our cozy family home

Those early years in Leipzig were filled with the simple joys of family life, of bike rides and walks in the park, of visits to my grandparents where the coffee table was set in the finest china and everyone dressed in their Sunday best. Their apartment was in a refined neighborhood and the interior was elegant with parquet floors and an oven of colorful tiles; a bench around it provided comfort and coziness.

I spent many hours with my father going to Sunday mass and stopping at his favorite shops for specialties to bring home. My brother Wolfgang, used to having his way, spent time with my mother who catered to all his wishes and to mine as well. Aunt Magda would say he is spoiled rotten and could not be taken anywhere. Often we would be asked to exit the streetcars; Wolfgang used the long benches as a slide and could not be stopped. So we would walk and he could climb the planters. He was a restless guest at the coffee table and he and Mami−our affectionate name for our mother−would often leave early. I stayed as long as I could to look at art books with Aunt Magda and be around her friends who were painters and dancers. They wore colorful clothes and smelled of exotic flowers.

As a family of four, we enjoyed bike rides. Small wicker baskets were attached to steering wheels. We rode on trails in parks, on soft sandy ground, stopping to take pictures with a box camera. I felt my father's big shoulders wrapped around me and wished the ride would never end. He was not a tall man, but to me he was strong and reliable. My father wore glasses and was bald, I saw him as smart and caring. He had married late in life, at the age of 45, after his parents had died and he was so proud of his young family who came first in his life.

I remember train rides to our vacation spot in the Ore mountains, often called Saxon Switzerland. We stayed in a guesthouse and walked the trails of the majestic forest which included massive pine trees, evergreens and deep green moss. This is where Ruebezahl lived, the mountain man all children believed in. We ate the simple food of the area, local fish mostly, and felt privileged to have such a rich life.

Wolfgang and I, two happy healthy children, c. 1942

The war did not impact our lives directly at this time. It was fought in far-away locations, in North Africa and on the Eastern and Western front. The air war had not yet started and the radio only mentioned Nazi victories in France and Poland.

German soldiers marching and performing "Heil Hitler", the Nazi salute in Germany

Changes to our lives happened slowly. There were a large number of uniformed police in the streets. Aunt Magda taught me how to avoid the Heil Hitler greeting that was due all uniformed men. We would move to the other side of the street, or we would drop something and be busy picking up the item, or she would scold me for misbehaving. A game at first, it turned serious in a short time

I remember one time when my Mother and I were walking home. We had picked daisies in the park which was not allowed and suddenly we saw two SS men approaching. My mother quickly tried to hide the flowers under her straw hat, but it was too late and we were taken to the police station. My mother had black curly hair and was always slightly tanned. She was petite and graceful and these police men treated her in a domineering, threatening, and controlling manner. My mother was afraid and I sensed her fear of these uniformed men in their polished outfits who treated us like criminals under their control for stealing flowers from a public park. I, too, was afraid and aware that changes were happening.

Grandfather had to be persuaded to not walk the streets in his neighborhood and not to speak loudly about his disdain for Hitler and his cohorts. Aunt Magda appeared anxious and worried. Her place of employment, a bookstore and publishing company, had been raided and the manager was removed by police, never to be seen again. In later years I learned the full story of the raid. The sermons of the local bishop, Graf von Galen, were kept in a drawer under the cash register and distributed to anyone who asked. The bishop himself was under house arrest and forbidden to preach because he had proclaimed Christian and anti-Nazi opinions.

Soon, food was rationed, meat and produce were in short supply. We children ate a lot of oatmeal and not only for breakfast. This once lively city was wrapped in darkness. It was mandatory to have black shades and to cover all windows at the first sign of darkness. My father was drafted in 1942, although he was 51 years old, and became a member of the Schutzpolizei, a special police force for the protection of the civilian population.

Aunt Magda would read the newspaper, or what was permitted to be printed, and my grandfather would raise his hands in anger and frustration. My father reacted with quiet restraint. Casual conversations in the stores and on the street were limited to close friends and relatives for fear of being reported. One day the concierge in our building talked to my mother about decorations for Hitler's birthday and her wish to have the whole house decorated. Days later, a warning was issued since no flags or pictures had appeared in our windows. All this happened as the three of us returned home from trying to shop for food. Still my mother's response was casual and non-committal.

Finally, the concierge made it clear that our family would be reported and the consequences would be severe. I heard my parents argue later and my mother's plea to do it for the children's sake. Soon there were tiny Nazi flags in our windows on the fifth floor and my father seemed old and tired. He had always been an unassuming man, not in need of wealth or recognition. He now had to make decisions that affected his faith, his political convictions and the safety of his family.

Example of Nazi flags that decorated the streets and homes in Germany during the Second World War

The people in Leipzig were mostly protestant, the few Catholics, my family included, belonged to the Catholic diaspora and congregated in the few parishes in and around the city. There was a special church on the outskirts of the city where we would usually celebrate the feast of Corpus Christi, a major Catholic holy day in Germany. On this day, the host is carried around in a procession to five altars, accompanied by all the treasures of the individual church followed by a brass band and by the congregation. This traditional religious celebration took on a different meaning, when SS troops surrounded the procession, taking notes and staring in silence at all who participated. It was the last open celebration of a religious feast in Leipzig until after the war.

Large cities like Hamburg and Berlin bore the brunt of heavy air attacks at first. Leipzig was bombed a short time later. It was my job to get dressed when the sirens warned of an imminent air raid, grab the bag of essential papers and walk down the winding staircase past the stained glass windows to the shelter in the basement. I did this with trepidation and anxiety for myself, for my mother and brother who were still on the top floor of the house and fear of the dark staircase ahead.

Allied bombers over Germany during World War II

One night, a bomb hit nearby and exploded, shattering the stained glass windows. Glass and stone were flying everywhere. The bag of family papers slipped out of my hands and rolled down the stairs. I screamed and ran back upstairs. I held on to my mother and cried that I would never go to the basement alone.

There were ruins all around and smoke and dust filled the air. I knew the sound airplanes made when they came closer and changed altitude to drop bombs. Wolfgang was young enough to sleep in the shelter, I cried in fear when bombs hit nearby and the walls were shaking.

One morning, as we emerged from the shelter, Muhme was there. My father informed us that she was here to stay, in our playroom, and we should be considerate of her. She had no home to go to, no place to live. Muhme did not speak our language; at least we did not understand her. Who was she?

We soon learned that my father, as a policeman, had found her hiding among the ruins. She had nothing but the clothes on her back, no papers, no rations, no form of ID. It was clear to my parents that she was hiding from the authorities and that her presence posed a danger to our family if she were discovered. My father did not share her identity with anyone, not even my mother. Muhme stayed in our apartment and never ventured outside. As children we had a hard time adjusting to her presence and she had little tolerance for us. When we were too noisy she would raise her fist at us and chase us away from her door yelling in her strange language.

In those days of heavy bombing, we slept in one room, three of us in my parents' big bed and Wolfgang in his crib.

He insisted that Mami hold his hand until he fell asleep and every time he woke up during the night. Sometimes I would ask that she hold my hand too, and sometimes she would, but not for long. I was the big sister and had to behave like one.

With my father in a park in Leipzig, c. 1943

In the early hours of December 4, 1943, the three of us emerged from the bomb shelter. The heaviest bombing of

Leipzig had just ended. The air was filled with smoke and dust, even inside the house. It was Wolfgang's fourth birthday. My mother had found a bag of colored building blocks and Wolfgang was so excited about his present. He brushed aside all tiredness and started to build all over the living room. No one was allowed near his buildings as he repeated over and over "no bombs, no bombs".

One day, after another destructive raid on the inner city, the whole family decided to leave and move temporarily to Wittichenau, a small town east of Leipzig where my grandmother was born and had family who would find temporary housing for all of us.

My father was eventually transferred to units in Prague. We left our big and beautiful apartment to a young mother and daughter who had lost all their belongings in an air raid and they in turn promised to keep Muhme safe who needed to stay out of sight.

I was making the trip with Aunt Magda. We left our apartment and had to walk to the city center because there were no streetcars in operation. My mouth was covered with a scarf because of the smoke. So many houses lay in ruin, some still smoldering, and my grandmother's church had been leveled. We made it to the formerly grand railroad station where one wing was still functioning and found our train to Wittichenau.

I was five years old. I had a teddy bear in my arms and I was scared for many reasons. My father was not with us and I could not imagine life without him. Leipzig was destroyed in so many places. I hoped that Aunt Magda would take me and all of us to a safe place.

* *

Historical Context:

On 9 November 1938, as part of Kristallnacht, in Gottschedstrasse (<u>German</u>: Gottschedstraße), now a popular dining and nightlife area in Leipzig, synagogues and businesses were set on fire. Only a few days later, on 11 November 1938, many Jews in the Leipzig area were deported to the Buchenwald Concentration Camp. As

World War II came to an end, much of Leipzig was destroyed. Following the war, the Communist Party of Germany *provided aid for the reconstruction of the city.*

Destruction in Leipzig during World War II

Chapter 2: Winter 1943- winter 1944: A short stay in friendly Wittichenau

Making a life in cramped conditions

Map of Germany; the pin is placed over Wittichenau, a small town east of Leipzig where we moved during the war.

Wittichenau, a small town in Lusatia, a section of Germany East of Saxony and West of Silesia, was our new home. The extended family of grandparents, three aunts and our family of three lived in Kirchgasse, in a small house on a narrow street. I remember a small garden in the back of the house, mostly for vegetable beds. There was no room for children to run or play. That created problems between young and old.

Wolfgang, all of four years old and used to free range, was too much for my aging grandfather. The three of us soon moved to a shabby apartment on the outskirts of town. It had a huge window and open space around it. We would cuddle near the window and Mami would sing the folksongs she knew and recite ballads.

It was at the end of 1943 when we moved. One year in Wittichenau changed our lives dramatically. My brother and I looked thin and pale when we arrived, no longer children who ate three meals a day, who had seen a pediatrician regularly and had their pictures taken in silk outfits by a professional photographer. But relatives with small gardens and others with grocery stores helped us regain strength. There was a childcare center nearby and it offered not just playtime with toys we no longer had, but also food.

Wolfgang and I, two emaciated children in Wittichenau, c. 1943

At the age of five, I was an alert and observant child. When I saw that kids were fed spinach against their will, force-fed by pinching their nostrils shut, I became the protective older sister, grabbed my four-year old brother's hand and together we ran home, never to return.

The winter passed slowly and Easter promised happiness as my father would be able to visit us. The days he spent with us were special. There was story time and quiet time. A few days before Easter he participated in a retreat for men ending with the traditional local Easter ride into the town.

The men arrived on horses as a reminder of Jesus' ride into Jerusalem and were greeted with applause and brass music. In Market Square, my father pulled me up on his horse and we rode around the square. I felt secure with his arms around me and his love for all of us.

Those were the last times I saw my father.

He would send us postcards, addressed to Fraulein Voigt and Herr Voigt, with pictures of all the places where he was stationed, and promises that he would travel with us everywhere. My mother received more sober letters that revealed his decision never to shoot another human being and his hope that she would raise us "in our joint conviction and faith".

It was many years later when we were teenagers that my mother shared these letters with us. Both of us felt that his obligation to be around us, his children, to provide food and shelter was greater than his moral belief. We both were hardened by many years of total deprivation.

One day as I was running home I saw a plane diving low and heading directly towards the bridge I was about to cross. I was frozen in fear, unable to move. It seemed forever as I stood there when strong arms grabbed me and pulled me to safety into a nearby field where we lay flat on the ground. For a long time, even after all war activity stopped, I felt compelled to hide when an airplane flew by.

Food became harder to get and we existed on cereal and bread. Many children were already ill when epidemics of scarlet fever and diphtheria broke out. All those with a sign of illness were hospitalized and homes were disinfected. My mother and aunt took me to the local hospital in a small hand-pulled wagon; there were no ambulance transports.

I remember a big room with beds of different sizes and kids of all ages from toddlers to teenagers; we all had scarlet fever. A small window was the only connection to the outside world. Parents would crowd around this tiny window to wave and throw kisses to their children. We all were eagerly awaiting the day that we would be allowed to go home. It did not happen. I developed pain in my joints and could not move. Instead a nurse carried me to another part of the hospital where I received treatment for rheumatic fever whatever treatment was available at the height of war in 1944. Now I occupied a room all by myself, a dark and gloomy room and curtains just as dark. I slept a lot and feared the visits from the lab to perform blood tests. There was all the food I could eat, sandwiches and cold cuts, eggs and potatoes, but all I wanted were the strawberries my mother would bring. She would roll me outside in a wheelchair and tell me fairy tales and time would pass.

Finally, one day in early August, after 6 weeks in the hospital, I was able to go home, happily anticipating the welcome I would receive from the whole family. When we opened the door to the house on Kirchgasse, there was only sadness, tears and cries, a torn telegram and my mother's moans.

I sat in the garden, alone, staring at the bright sunny August sky and wished I had never come home to hear that my father was gone. We walked home later that day, my mother and I. The sky was still bright with barely a cloud. We did not talk and we did not cry. I knew I would never look at a sunny sky without remembering this day in August when my world lost its brightness. I wanted the whole world to show the sadness I felt, I wanted the sky to be dark, the town to be dirty, people to be ugly and mean. But I was just quiet.

As I later learned, my father was standing watch in Warsaw on the first day of the Polish uprising and was one of the first to fall. He was buried in the German "Heldenfriedhof" (hero cemetery), over the objections of my mother who wanted him returned home for a Christian burial. Her wishes were ignored. None of us were allowed to visit Warsaw in the postwar years and later the need to see my father's grave diminished.

As a teenager, going to school in Bamberg, I met a daughter of Colonel von Stauffenberg, the man who had attempted to assassinate Hitler by placing a bomb in his bunker. He was not successful and was shot for this courageous deed. We talked about our losses and wondered how our lives would have been different if her father in his attempt on July 20th, 1944 had succeeded and lived, Hitler would have been killed and my father, ten days later in Warsaw, would have survived.

Claus von Stauffenberg, the man who had attempted to assassinate Hitler, and was later shot for this deed.

In first grade, at least in the early months of first grade, school lasted only two or three hours. Quite often, an alarm sounded for an imminent air strike and we had to leave school and run home since the school had no shelter.

I was quiet in school and did not actively participate. It was not shyness or lack of knowledge. The teacher asked if I ever spoke at home because she had never heard my voice. I felt sad and removed from everyday activities and did not want to learn to read or write. Bombing raids were happening during the day in this rural area when the planes returned from larger targets and sometimes dropped their last bombs nearby.

I feared for the safety of my mother and brother who often took bike rides in the country. An airplane had dumped a bomb on a group of children who were on a field trip. Was it planned, was it an accident? The people in Wittichenau were wondering.

Soon thereafter a British airplane went down in a nearby field, the pilot landed safely with his parachute. There was a lot of anger in this small town for all the destruction and the attack on children. The pilot became a scapegoat. He was paraded through main street in his brown uniform and white socks. People lined the streets and threw apples and stones at him, some called for execution.

He was soon forgotten in the commotion and turmoil of a war that was coming closer and closer to civilian life or what was left of it.

In early 1945 air attacks continued and Dresden was fire-bombed. The Russians troops were advancing through Poland and into Germany. News spread by word of mouth through the many refugees and people on the move in advance of the Russian army who brought a wave of destruction, of land, property and life wherever they set foot.

Millions of people formed the Red Flood, this stream of refuges moving from East to West. They came from Rumania, Bulgaria, Ukraine, from Poland and the German provinces in the east. They all hoped to save their lives by meeting the Allied Forces.

They told stories of plundering troops who took not only property, but raped, tortured and murdered. Their stories were repeated over and over. In East Prussia, a farmer who was trying to protect his property was nailed to his barn door while his wife was able to hide under the hay bundles. Many years later, I was told about a mother who stood on a bridge in Vienna with her two teenage daughters urging them to jump together into the water of the Danube to escape the advancing Russians. The girls were too strong and refused.

Crimes diminished as the Russian Army came closer to American troops; yet even in Berlin when Eisenhower and his soldiers were less than 100 miles from the city, women were raped and jumped out of windows to escape.

One of the last groups of refugees coming through Wittichenau were the Cossacks. They came with wild horses pulling covered wagons and they were asking for huge amounts of money and desperate people were glad to pay as my family was.

We decided to join the stream of refugees. It was an easy decision since we had no property in Wittichenau. Farmers and small businesses had a hard time leaving all this behind. My family was different. The few things of value were packed in large trunks and buried in the ground with the help of family and neighbors. We never saw our property again and never returned to Wittichenau.

It was a difficult journey. Wolfgang clutched his teddy bear, the only toy he possessed. Grandfather stood upright in the wagon which was covered in a simple linen cloth; I thought it might have been too hard for him to get down and sit on the bottom of the wagon and then try to get up again. Or was he giving his seat to Grandmother? My mother rode with us on a different wagon and sold all her jewelry so we could have more blankets.

When we approached the area south of Leipzig, another decision had to be made. We could return to our homes which were still standing despite numerous bombings, or continue further west where American soldiers were more likely to be; they might treat us better than Russians.

In wartime Germany, the truth was difficult to find. Warnings spoke of war crimes by all, whether American, British, French or Russian. We chose to continue through the mountain ranges in the center of Germany. Areas like Saxony and Thuringia led us finally into the northern areas of Bavaria. Our journey with the Cossacks ended in Lichtenfels where local police were present to handle the influx of people moving East to West. This enormous migration of people who feared the Red Army would prove to be justified; the Red Army destroyed property, robbed and raped and took whatever pleased them.

During World War II, some 25 million Soviet citizens served in the armed forces of USSR, mostly in the Red Army. The Red Army is considered the largest land force that allowed Allied victory in the European fronts. Little is mentioned about the torture they enforced on Germans during their "successful invasions"

* *

Historical Context:

Nazi censorship assured that my family and I knew nothing when, on June 6, 1944, 155,000 Allied troops landed on the beaches of Normandy in France. The Allied soldiers quickly broke through German defenses and pushed inland in the largest amphibious military operation in history.

Chapter 3: 1944−1964: We escape to Bavaria and start a new life

An oasis of peace amid chaos

Lichtenfels is a small town in northeastern Bavaria; only a detailed map of the area would show its name. Local police guided us to shelters and private homes. We spent a night with a family who shared their home and their food with the three of us, and provided an oasis of peace after our difficult journey. Their son, a boy about twelve years old, showed me his room where he had built an altar so that he could say prayers for his family and all of us in need of help.

It was a simple row house, sitting just a few feet off the street, we slept on couches and benches and yet felt embedded in luxury and caring love. I wanted to stay in this house forever, it meant rest and peace.

In early 1945, most towns were already filled with refugees from big cities like Hamburg, Cologne and Frankfurt which had been destroyed in air raids. There was only room in the remote countryside. The next day we moved on, across country roads another 15 miles, accompanied by German police, to a small village of about 30 farm houses high up in the Jura mountains. The bus stopped at various houses and the police would talk to the homeowners and request that the farmers take us in. It took a good deal of persuasion and sometimes force before they would open their doors and restrain their dogs.

These farm houses were already filled to capacity and they had no heating in any of their upstairs rooms. We were assigned to a house where another refugee family already lived. Together there were now two mothers and five children living in a shared kitchen and two bedrooms. A stove with a long vent to the outside provided a primitive heat source and cooking facility in the kitchen. The bedrooms were not heated and we all had to use one drop toilet. Most refugee families were not any better off. All farmers and their children slept in cold bedrooms; the cows in the stable on the first floor of the house helped in the coldest nights.

Burkheim is situated in the mountainous area between Bamberg and Bayreuth. In 1945 it was a village of about 30 houses lining the main road which at this time was muddy, full of potholes and torn up by military vehicles. Most houses belonged to farmers. There were two beer breweries, one of them served as a temporary school and there were smaller houses that belonged to a cobbler, a plumber, a woodworker and a blacksmith. There were no privately owned cars and the one bus that provided a connection to the nearest town operated only occasionally. Bicycles were the mode of transportation between small villages and larger towns like Altenkunstadt and Burgkunstadt. Only a few farmers had horses that were used mostly for farm work and the carriages came out of the barn for special occasions only.

For adults, it was as safe a place as one could hope for in this time of continuing war. I was seven years old and lost.

Mountains, for me, were dangerous and restrictive. I longed for the wide-open sky of the flat land where I had grown up and where I could see far into the distance. I wanted parks and paved roads, manicured lawns and flowers growing in beds. Most of all, I wanted my father.

There were those red tennis shoes. They were the only nice thing I owned. I do not remember where they came from. Lying on my straw mattress and holding them in my hands I insisted on wearing them outside. My mother said no, the streets are muddy and you will ruin them. My temper tantrum was long and fierce and contained all the hardships of the last weeks, the present deprivation and limitation and all the difficulties ahead. By the time the weather had warmed up and the streets were dry, I had outgrown those memorable red tennis shoes.

Not long after our arrival in Burkheim, a school delegate contacted my mother and reminded her that I had to attend school which was held in the local inn. It was early 1945 and signs of war, of shooting, bombing and explosions were not far away. I went to school only once and realized it consisted largely of Nazi propaganda songs and poems in praise of Hitler. Being well trained by my father and aunt I refused to go back to school, screaming and crying and thus, in the last days of war, my small protest prevailed.

There were more explosions and occasionally tanks and jeeps would drive through. Roads and bridges were being destroyed by the retreating German troops in order to stop the advance of the Allied troops. A small group of soldiers, a sergeant and young soldiers, boys really, with their truck and tank, stopped in the neighbor's yard. They intended to set up a defense position right there in the middle of this small remote area. Kids gathered around them, smelling the food from their canteen and stared at the strange activity.

The sergeant was somehow persuaded by the mayor, a fellow farmer, to look for a better place to fight. I stood across the street and watched. One of the young soldiers motioned for me to come over and then offered me his soup. I happily ate and thanked him. It was then that I saw the sadness, the fear and the tears in his eyes. The small group moved on to the next village where they took one last stand. A battle ensued, many lives were lost and the village destroyed.

In the following weeks, a few more German soldiers came through Burkheim. These did not look like soldiers, more like lost souls, weary and disheveled, not seeking any confrontation. They were hiding from the war just like we were. But they came with a warning to hide from the advancing American troops. So we hid in the caves that had been built in the woods as storage places. After a few days and little food, we returned to the village. More news through word of mouth reduced our fears of the American Army that was approaching rapidly. We started to believe that an end to the war was coming and civilians might not be killed randomly.

The first American soldiers come through the streets of Burkheim in tanks and open jeeps. They were smiling. They threw chewing gum to us children who stood behind the fences and we promptly swallowed it. It was food. Thus the liberation and occupation of Germany began.

American tanks moving through a destroyed German city, with smiling soldiers at the end of World War II

The impact on our lives was minimal at first. Burkheim was not important or large enough to house a contingent of the US army. There was one intense search for an SS member who was believed to be hiding in the woods. Jeeps ran through fields and woods in search of him. He was the father of three children I knew and I was concerned for them. He was quickly caught and soon released as unimportant. Another girl with older sisters would tell us wondrous tales about nylons, cans of meat, cocoa and real coffee that her older sisters would bring home. It took a few years for me to understand the reason for these miraculous gifts and why the family was shunned.

Many years later, when I was attending school in Bamberg and learning English, I was asked to help the mayor of Burkheim who had a visitor. It was a black man, a former soldier who had returned from the United States to look for his son and the son's mother. I translated the story to the mayor. He then asked me to take the man to the place where his son and son's mother were known to live. It was an old house high up on the mountain.

My aunt was uneasy about this long hike with a man we did not know and decided to accompany us. We walked through fields and meadows and when we reached the forest, Aunt Madga could not keep pace. So the two of us walked on and he told me about his life in America and the home he had created for himself in the hope of bringing his son and the mother to a good place.

But a lot of time had passed, life had changed for everyone. I left the man at the old farmhouse where he waited. I heard that he left the area after a few days, alone. The boy, his son, did not know him, did not speak English and had no interest in leaving familiar surroundings; neither did his mother who planned on marrying a farmer and build a rest stop or coffee shop on the now very popular mountain.

In May 1945, the war was finally over and the people around me were relieved, tired and hungry. Now the aftermath of war and destruction was apparent. The worst part, for me and my family, was the lack of food and the isolation in this remote region. We had nowhere to go, no toys, no clothes except the dirty ones on our back, no friends. Many people were ill with the flu and with skin infections and digestive problems

The population of Burkheim had doubled in the last months of the war. There were people from many regions; most were German people who had lost their homes to bombs. Others came from eastern areas, where Russia had annexed a huge part of Poland and in exchange given Poland the German areas east of the Oder/Neisse rivers. Some of the refugees spoke a different language. Most spoke a different dialect, but all had escaped the Red Army.

We felt like foreigners in this remote area and the farmers treated us as like strangers from an unknown land; most newcomers understood nothing of farm life, of fields or meadows or farm animals. My mother was referred to as the "black one" because of her pitch black hair and my Grandfather was mocked as he shuffled along the street in his suit and vest, the only clothes he possessed.

Roosevelt's advisors had urged him to make Germany into a strictly agricultural land to avoid any future wars. The British were eager to receive all the industrial equipment and technical advantages; they had suffered so much damage in this ugly war. The Russians wanted land, as much of the Eastern part of Germany as possible. They got their wish when American troops who under General Eisenhower had advanced to within 100 km of Berlin, retreated and instead traded the central part of Germany, which included Saxony, for West Berlin which in the post-war years would be the cause of East/West disagreements until the fall of the wall in 1989. It meant for us that

Leipzig, once safely in American hands, would now be part of the Russian-controlled area.

These deals created problems for our lives in 1945. The food produced by German farmers could not feed the large population that had nearly doubled. Living in the country we begged for food and learned the local custom of always saying "Vergelt es Gott" (God's reward) and hearing the customary answer "Segen es Gott" (God Bless it). A piece of bread had to last a long time. Most people carried an old hard piece of bread in their coat pocket and chewed on it whenever hungry without consuming a lot of it.

Coal was hard to get. The coal mines were in British and French hands and others in Soviet possession. We collected wood in the forests and my Mother became an expert in splitting the big logs that would not fit our wood-fired cooking stove. To have wood, small kindling and larger logs meant being rich and well equipped to survive the cold winter. Coal would have lasted longer and kept the room warm at night. The Cardinal of Cologne declared that stealing in order to survive was not a sin but a necessity in these difficult situations.

As children, we adjusted gradually to life in the country. We learned the local dialect and communicated with local kids. We acted as interpreters between our family members and the locals and soon we spoke the rural dialect. It was almost a new language. There was no room for us indoors. Our grandparents were forced to move in with us and there was but one heated room. My brother was too noisy and unruly for grandfather and arguments happened daily. There were no toys, no games, no books. Often we stayed in bed to keep warm and to stay out of trouble.

Spring came late that year and life became easier. We explored the countryside and found much to see in this mountainous area. There was a hill on one side called Weinberg, where vineyards once might have stood, now there were mostly fruit trees, meadows and a forest perfect for strawberries and blueberries. It became our favorite place for sledding. A dark forest of enormous pines on the other side always reminded me of Grimm's Haensel and

Gretel; we would not go there alone despite all the blueberries and mushrooms.

Tucked in between the woods was a very small place called Tauschendorf, a few small houses in an area smaller than Burkheim and so remote that no map ever listed it. One place that was famous was the largest mountain in the area, called Kordigast; poems were written about its beauty. It was covered in evergreen trees and in the following years we would hike up to the top on many occasions. The view was spectacular and showed the natural beauty of this part of the country, fields and meadows in a perfect geometric patterns of endless forests, softly rolling hills and not one acre unattended. Around this mountain we centered most of our activities in the next years, gathering wood, grains, mushrooms and berries.

Kordigast, Burkheim

All this took years to discover and explore. At the end of WWII we were lucky to be outside and not in fear. We picked flowers and collected wood for the oven. My mother saw an opportunity to provide food for her family when she was offered the chance to start a collection station of snails for American soldiers who had acquired a taste for them in France. A small shed on the farm was used to hold a scale and plenty of buckets. The snails were brought in by anyone who wished to be part of this business and my mother weighed them and paid everyone accordingly. I was one of the exceptions; I never picked up a snail, never ate one and had nightmares about this huge pile of slimy beasts in the shed not far from the house.

During the first summer a serious threat endangered the food supply. It was the potato bug that surfaced for the first time on German farms and threatened to destroy the yearly crop. Without the expected potato harvest there was no way to feed the massive population. American soldiers organized a huge group of able adults, mostly women, to walk through the fields to collect and destroy the bugs and so the potato crop was saved. I remember sitting on the sidelines and watching my mother and my aunts walk through the rows in shoes that were ill-suited for this task and often just taking them off. In the end, everyone was pleased and the question where the bugs came from was never settled.

A temporary school opened in an old house; a teacher was selected who had no credentials, yet for us children it was a blessing. We went to school eager to learn, even without books and writing paper. Instead we used wrapping paper and the edges of newspapers.

School also meant food, cereal and soup and an abundance of grapefruit juice, which was unknown in the Germany and so the eager cooks mixed it in with the cereal, a dubious combination. Often there were leftovers of food and we could take it home. My grandfather was grateful for every little bite. Once, I saw him take a spoonful from Wolfgang's plate. I was prepared to scream in protest but stopped in time and never mentioned it to anyone. I was sad and ashamed.

Medical care was hard to find. Doctors had not returned from the war yet. A farmer was kicked by his unruly horse and there was no surgeon to help him recover. Women in labor delivered at home and often without the help of a midwife; they would cry out in pain. Skin infections, boils and furuncles were treated with certain plants that grew in the meadows. Children and older people had the hardest time overcoming the flu and pneumonia and so my grandfather was taken to the nearest hospital and never returned. He was buried on the same day as a well-off merchant and the merchant's family invited us to be part of their meal after the church service. It was an overwhelming act of kindness and thus refugees and locals came to know and tolerate each other.

My mother adapted quickly to her new life. She was the only one in our family who could control the vicious watchdog at the front entrance to the farmhouse and she had to let everyone else in and out of the house. She learned where best to find firewood. She taught us children where to be useful and so earn a piece of bread or an egg. She would flirt with the farmer where we lived in order to get a piece of bread or milk. But there was one enemy she had in Burkheim, namely geese. She would walk through the village with the biggest stick she could find to fend off the vicious gander.

As a child I did not look at my mother as special; it took a lot of years to see how hard it must have been for her, at the age of 46, to adjust to a totally new life. She did adjust and managed to feed her children and raise them as best as possible. At the same time, she must have had hopes and dreams for herself that were never realized in the remote countryside during the difficult post war years. Instead, my brother and I were concerned with our own lives and future.

We made friends with other refugee children; the farmers' children did not have much time to play, and instead we explored the fields and woods. Then we saw the "crooked tree", a tree growing almost parallel to the road with early apples. We shook the tree until many fell to the ground. Suddenly, the owner of the apple tree saw us and raced over in his wagon pulled by a horse and started to swing his whip at us giving us a good beating. All of us learned a hard and painful lesson which we never forgot while living in Burkheim: You can take what has fallen to the ground but never touch what hangs on the branches. That was true for all fruit trees.

My first job at the age of seven was to walk a sheep, to lead it by the leash to a meadow and let it feed while I sat in the grass. I had to be alert at all times or the sheep would take off and so I earned a big piece of farm bread with homemade cottage cheese. In the summer we learned where berries were growing, blueberries mostly, and bread, milk and berries became our daily food. Soon we discovered the spots where mushrooms would sprout, especially after a shower, which improved our daily diet considerably.

A boy carried a sack with newborn kittens around telling us kids that he would drown them. I grabbed one kitten and carried it home. I wanted to save it, feed it, carry it around and love it forever. Soon there were problems. My Omi, German for grandmother, almost fell because the little creature would not lie still in bed with me but wander around. There was the question of milk, of cleaning up after the kitten and so I had to return it to the original owner with tears in my eyes.

It took a long time for our school to take shape. Qualified teachers were hard to find; they had to have a clean background, meaning no participation in Nazi activities. I started second grade having attended first grade for a short time only and I could not read or write. The local children thought I was a dummy since I knew nothing useful, neither for school nor for farm life. I also was traumatized by air raids and would hide or throw myself to the ground anytime I heard an airplane.

It was a hard way to start school and make friends. With the help of my Aunt Magda I spent hours after school to catch up. After working hard for a few weeks, I was not only equal to other second graders; now the teacher wanted me to skip a grade and move into third grade. Again, I was stubborn and refused.

The following years brought little change. Our food supply was still limited to bread, milk and our own supply of berries and mushrooms. One mother who had escaped the bombs in Hamburg with her three children sold all her silver and valuable porcelain for food. My mother and aunts crossed the border to the Russian occupied area several times to bring back valuables from our home, but were always caught by Russian guards and robbed of their belongings. Luckily, they were not harmed.

In those early post-war years, the Western Allies, the US, Great Britain and France could find no agreement with the Russians on how to govern occupied Germany and so there was a division, the West which was jointly managed by the three Western nations and the Russian Zone. More and more people had fled from east to west and added to overcrowding and more food shortages. The Russian zone had more agricultural land and more coal. They needed a larger population and wanted to prevent more people from leaving. As a result, the "Iron Curtain" (so named by Winston Churchill) came down, a border guarded by Russian soldiers in the center of Germany.

The Iron Curtain Trail, a no-man's land that we had to cross to go from Burkheim to Leipzig in order to retrieve our belongings.

Burkheim was a small quiet place in a poor region tucked in between mountains, on a rural road and not too far from the border to East Germany. The fear of Russians never left us. At the end of WWII the population had increased dramatically and so did the need for food, for housing and roads, for transportation and schools. None of these were available. Burkheim was not different from other areas in Germany; we were just more isolated and had to help ourselves.

Frau P. was a prominent citizen who had enforced Nazi rules and propaganda during the war. She was used to running a bar full of men, serving beer and keeping it peaceful. She was a forceful woman and demanded respect. She and her family owned the brewery, an inn with guest rooms and also a bowling alley and a dance hall on their property. The village people shunned her at the end of the war by boycotting her pub. Instead, they would gather at a smaller pub with inferior beer and they elected a new mayor not endorsed by her.

But Frau P. had another side which became apparent when she took three refugee families into her guest house. One family with three children who were seriously neglected as their Mother proved unable to care for them, was totally under the care of Frau P. who fed them, dressed them and made sure they attended school and did their homework. In a few years, she was forgiven by the locals and her pub was again a favorite gathering place.

Burkheim at its best

In these post-war years, I adjusted to life in Burkheim and learned to appreciate the countryside for all its natural beauty. I admired a farm with old and original stucco. It was later declared a protected landmark. The walls were bulging slightly, but overall its beauty was still visible. All the farms had dirt courtyards for cows and horses to enter and wagons of hay and fresh grass to be unloaded. Barns and outbuildings formed a rectangle with the house. The waste pile was usually located in the back of the house and not visible from the front. Its smell no longer bothered me.

The fall of 1946 was a low point in our lives. President Truman thought the situation in West Germany could not last without a drastic solution: He ordered everyone who came from the Eastern part of Germany, the Russian occupied area, to return to their place of residence at the time WWII began. Our family refused to live under Russian occupation and so we stayed in Burkheim, part of Bavaria, part of the American sector. We received no rations and had very little to eat as winter approached. We cooked sugar beets until they were syrup and spread the syrup on the leftover bread, no matter how hard.

The farmers had to turn over their harvest to be picked up by collection agents and seemed to have enough left to feed their family only. These were small farms and some farmers only had cows to pull the plows or wagons. There were no tractors, the grass to feed the cows was cut with a scythe as was the rye and all other grains. With so many refugees in the village there was no extra food to share.

In desperation, my mother walked with us kids to a village more remote than Burkheim. We begged and were given bread and even a small sausage and said the customary "Thank God". I was a shy girl, almost eight years old and ashamed of begging. My brother, almost two years younger, smiled and melted many hearts. Then came the long walk home, food wrapped in old newspapers. It was a hard journey and became nearly impossible when it started to snow. We sat for a long while on the snowy mountain getting tired and sleepy. Wolfgang and I cried; we only wanted to rest and not move. My mother rose and angrily urged us on with reminders of all the food we had been given and could eat when we were home. It was a long walk and we never attempted this trip again, no matter how hungry we were.

Christmas came and we sat around our table close to the oven, my grandmother, my mother and her two sisters and my brother and I. It was quiet, no one complained or cried.

There was a knock on the door and Eva, the woman of the farm, never one to welcome us, entered with a big basket full of food, the kind we had not seen or even heard of, bacon and bread, Stollen, a German Christmas specialty, and apples for all. It was the best Christmas present ever.

Eventually, Truman relented and lifted the order. Not many people had left to live in the Soviet zone. But quite a few people resorted to theft. There were reports of missing animals, even dogs and cats and as children we were afraid to be out in the dark.

Many trips to retrieve part of our belongings from Leipzig were made by my mother and her sister. Crossing the Iron Curtain, now a no-man's land that was heavily guarded, was dangerous and if caught by Russian soldiers, life threatening. One time, I travelled with my Mother and Aunt Magda in search of a new and safer route to Leipzig. We first stopped in Frankfurt where we waited for the next train in the once magnificent train station. It was now just a shell, no roof, no place to sit, full of desperate people. There was no food or water. We finally caught a train to

Cologne that had to cross a valley on a temporary track with wooden supports only, no railing. Everyone on the train held their breath in fear and I was more afraid than ever before. I declared firmly that I would never cross that dangerous stretch again.

My Mother and Aunt Magda crossed the border to go to Leipzig while I stayed with my aunt Lisa, a nun, who worked in a lung sanatorium. No one was too concerned that I might pick up tuberculosis. Everyone was happy for me because in this place they had all the food imaginable, bread and cheese, sausage and other meats, mushrooms and vegetables and even cakes and cookies. There was music and I danced with many of the patients. For two weeks, I ate and slept well. Before returning home, on a different route that was considered safer, the nuns found a piece of white material, and thus made it possible for me to have a dress made and go to First Communion just like the farmers' kids. Life was good.

In 1949 school was real. We had two new teachers, one taught grades 1 to 4 and the other grades 5 to 8. I started grade 5 and was not used to serious study. It had all been a game so far. I had no school books like the other children and learned the hard way that I had to borrow books and study days ahead of everyone else so I would be prepared when the teacher called on me. In those years it felt good to impress my family and my teacher.

German prisoners of war returned slowly, but only those held by Allied Forces. Many were wounded and still healing, many were crippled, others were unable to forget what they had seen. A local farmer came home and was eager to resume farm work despite missing a shoulder. He was happy to be home, to smell the fresh air and feed his animals. One man came through the village with a cart and offered to sharpen knives and one was able to fix the holes in pots and pans, a much needed service. One man was a tailor and promised to turn men's suits into women's suits. For many years, one could see women in suits in our part of the country; their shoulders were huge and their jackets long and everyone knew who had been the tailor and where the material came from.

We quietly mocked these war widows. In those days it was not important what one looked like. My mother would wear her skirt with a blouse in the summer and the whole suit all other seasons for quite a few years. The tailor had an indentation on his head, covered by skin only, an obvious war injury. It would pulsate with his heartbeat and as children we were both fascinated and repulsed.

Our family, my mother and her two children, our extended family of grandmother and two aunts was still poor and lived in two rooms per family, without running water and heat only in the kitchen. But we learned to love life in the country. I picked berries with my friends and for my friends who made jam.

One of my proudest moments came when the thrashing machine came to our farmer and we were asked to help with throwing the bundles of grain from the rafters down to the men who were feeding the machine. We climbed like monkeys high up in the rafters of the barn rolling the rye, the wheat and the barley to the farmer who would open the bundles and hand them to the man in front of the machine.

Others would fill the sacks and carry the grain into the house.

*Wolfgang, third from the left and I am fourth.
We, along with a few other children, are helping with the
grain, c. 1950*

At lunchtime there were bowls of water with soap and towels and after washing up, everyone entered the dining room where a huge table was set with many chairs and food for all, meat and dumplings, sausages and potatoes. The farmer's wife pulled out a chair for me to sit with all the grown-ups at the big table and told me that it was well deserved. I was immensely proud and wanted to live forever on a farm.

The potato harvest provided another opportunity to help. After the farmer turned the rows over with horse and plow, we would pick the potatoes, collect them in a large basket and carry the basket to the wagon where they were put in sacks. We again earned a place at the adult table and ate heartily. As a result, my mother had all the potatoes she wanted for the whole year.

School became more serious with a new teacher. My brother was sent to a boarding school to attend "Gymnasium", a school similar to prep school. At ten years old in 1949, he was homesick and lonely. I helped to establish the new library in our elementary school and read almost every book. The teacher kept urging my mother to send me away to school and Aunt Magda would not stop talking about the importance of higher education for women. When I passed all entrance exams with flying colors, I finally was sent to boarding school in Bamberg.

Education was free for both us; we were considered war orphans, and boarding school was necessary since we lived so far away in the country. The only problem was the lack of money for all other expenses. My new friends in Bamberg came from different backgrounds. They were the daughters of doctors and dentists or came from families with commercial holdings. They were visited by parents in fancy cars and taken to expensive restaurants. They had lots of dresses and matching shoes and, at teatime, our afternoon break from studying, they ate the special food sent from home. I missed the simple life of farming and eating what we had harvested. I missed my friends and life in Burkheim.

Bamberg at its best. This is the Old Rathaus, a World Heritage site in Bamberg

After each trimester, we would return home to the two rooms in the farm house. My mother would meet us at the train station and load our suitcases full of dirty laundry onto her bike and we would walk about an hour to reach home. There we climbed the mountains and walked in the woods searching for mushrooms. But friendships slowly faded; we were different, we spoke differently and were no longer children but growing up with different goals in life.

Near the Farm in Burkheim, c. 1954
This was our last year in Burkheim while going to school in Bamberg

At the end of the first school year, I found a job at the local pottery factory. An old bike took me to work every day but

Sunday. I made some money, enough to buy a dress for the new school year. Wolfgang and a local friend followed my example the next summer. Earning a meal or potatoes was no longer our primary goal. In the eyes of the farmer's children, though, we were now factory workers whom they looked at with disdain. Working the land and taking care of animals was far superior.

In 1954, at age 16, I found a job in Bamberg and earned more money while attending school. The housing situation improved slightly at that time and we located a place to live close to Bamberg. It was an improvement but we still shared a bathroom with another family and had only one living space.

I think my mother had a hard time leaving Burkheim where she had spent so many years and also leaving her mother and sister. A farmer loaded her three pieces of furniture onto a truck and drove her to her new location. She had loved the mountains, the forests, the clean air, vegetables and fruits so readily available. The noise of the city bothered her and so did the traffic.

My First job as a teacher, c. 1962

The area of Bamberg eventually became home. My mother, finally, 25 years after the end of WWII, had again all the conveniences of modern life. My brother became a representative for publishing companies and earned a generous living. I finished school and college and became a first grade teacher in a small town near Bamberg. After that I was employed by the US Army Education Center and taught German language courses to army members. In this job, I met my husband, an infantry officer who had been sent to Germany in response to the building of the Berlin Wall, and we married in 1963. After his duty was over, we came to Pittsburgh with our first child and I have lived here ever since.

When I left Bamberg in 1964 with my American family of three I did not know that I would miss this area so much and so I happily return as often as possible.

* *

Historical Context:

On May 7, 1945, the new German president, Admiral Karl Dönitz, authorized the unconditional surrender of the armed forces of Nazi Germany to the Allies. The next day, May 8, became Victory In Europe (VE) day in the United States.

Chapter 4: I return to Leipzig

After the war ended I found a few new buildings, others in ruins, many bullet holes, and polluted air and water

I returned to Leipzig a few more times. As a student in 1952, I spent about ten days of Easter vacation with an aunt who had remained in the area and worked for a parish on the outskirts of Leipzig. This trip was an adventure and a history lesson for me.

I boarded a train with a visa from the East German government and a few grocery items, like coffee, cocoa and chocolates hidden in my luggage. We passed the West German border station where our papers were checked and final instructions were issued and then the train moved across a strip of No Man's Land, the Iron Curtain, to the East German border and police. A loudspeaker announced

"You have entered the German Democratic Republic". The atmosphere was tense with questions for each passenger and reasons for the trip. A few people were removed from the train, some in handcuffs. I tried to remember what my mother had said; the worst they can do to you is to take your goodies and send you back home. But I had no problems.

The so-called German Federal Republic was not a democracy, but part of the Soviet Block and totally under Russian control, just like Czechoslavia, Hungary, Poland and all the countries that Russia had annexed after WWII. One could enter with a Visa if the Russians considered the purpose of the visit legitimate. No Americans were allowed to cross the border. In the years following, many East Germans attempted to flee across the border between East and West Germany or across the Berlin Wall, and many were killed.

In Leipzig, I remembered the train station. It had not been restored to its old glory. I remembered the house where we had lived, the parks, the wide open streets. There was one distinctive change: all looked gray and dirty, the houses, the streets, the people in their worn outfits. Ruins remained everywhere.

I found the opera house. I found Thomaskirche and Felsenkeller, my father's favorite restaurant.

The East German government was managing a bank account for my mother, from my father's estate, and allowed the family access to the money only while we were in the East zone. The amount in the bank account was close to 1 Million East marks; that was about 300,000 in West German currency. I could have spent in abundance if only there was something to buy. I found a petticoat, after standing in line for hours. I found books, mostly Russian authors and those with Communist leanings. I went to the opera, a grand production of Turandot.

My brother and I made the same trip a few years later. We saw it as the only vacation we could afford since we could use the money in the bank for everyday expenses. At another time my mother travelled with me. Leipzig did not change much in those years, a few high rises of utilitarian style went up around the university, but the air was dirty and the buildings reflected it.

Many years had passed, when the wall came down in 1989, not just the Berlin wall but also the wall between East and West Germany. Living in the United States, so far away, I was moved to tears of happiness seeing the faces of those who were now free. It was a miracle.

My brother started the process of regaining what we had lost. The bank account was never found. One of my visits, a few years later, stirred my memory and I identified the corner lot where my Grandfather's factory had stood, now in shambles. We were able to gain possession of the lot and sold it to a local man who wanted to build a garage. It was a small amount, not the fortune we had expected.

Grandfather's old window factory in ruins, c. 1992
This is the only property we could claim after reunification

It is only now, after reunification so many years later, that Leipzig and other cities in the east of Germany have regained beauty and value.

Leipzig is again a cultural center with a large university, a top-ranked orchestra and a famous book fair. The Rathaus still contains the records that the KGB collected of its citizens. One of the most famous KGB officials who worked in Leipzig during the cold war was Vladimir Putin, the current President of Russia.

Epilogue: A Note from Peter Day

My mom's story is one of courage, immigration and the strength of women that I'm delighted that others can now experience by virtue of this long-overdue memoir.

The indelible mark left on me throughout my own childhood was the courage displayed by my mother. How she was able to handle the trials that she faced in her American life—from a permanently troubled marriage, death of her daughter, several heart surgeries stemming from the childhood untreated Scarlet Fever and many others—has always astounded me. Now the readers of this memoir can appreciate the profound struggles of her upbringing and how it steeled her to endure and ultimately overcome the pains that awaited her in America. That these unique challenges did not overwhelm her is a testament to her undeniable courage and resilience.

Brigitta with her children, Tina and Peter, c. 1973

In today's United States, immigration is one of the more divisive political topics. This story reminds us of the pains that many immigrants endure–painful childhoods without many simple joys, the difficult journey with both physical and mental pains that endure for a lifetime, the challenges in reestablishing a 'normal life' in the new land, and the complex feelings of both compassion and distrust people can have at incoming strangers. Throughout my life and even today, my mom is culturally different from many of those in the families with whom I grew up. My childhood treats included goose fat on pumpernickel and escargot. Festive meals were duck and goose. My favorite food is Koenigsberger Klops, same as my kids now. I'm hard pressed to find anyone who had these meals in their home growing up. I proudly carry on many of these traditions (okay, not the goose fat) today because they both remind me of my happy childhood but also honor my heritage.

The sheer will of the women and their refusal to succumb in this story is an inspiration to us all. My mom's mother, who I called Omi, was a tiny woman—5 feet tall and less than 100 pounds—yet she was able to lead the family of two children, her two sisters, one of which had special needs, and of course her elderly father to a place of safety, and then to raise them on basically a sustenance living while educating them. Today we talk about 'home schooling' and challenges the world is facing in this regard. How about trying 'road schooling' when you are walking across your country filled with grief from the husband/father being killed in a war none of them wanted with no food and no guided instruction by a teacher via Zoom? I did not meet Omi until she was in her 70s, but she was as formidable as she was kind, generous and loving.

My hope is that readers of this memoir will take away feelings of hope, resilience, compassion and courage–characteristics that I witnessed in abundance growing up.

– Peter Day

Made in the USA
Monee, IL
18 February 2021